Your Definitive Guide to Decorative Fruit & Vegetable Carving for All Occasions!

By Francine Agile

Table of Contents

Copyright 4
Introduction 6
Chapter 1: The History of Food Carving 7
    Fruit and Vegetable Carving 8
    Ice Carving 9
    Tibetan Food Carving 10
    History of Vegetable Carving 11
    Japanese Vegetable Carving 11
    Thai Vegetable Carving 12
    Chinese Fruit Carving 13
    European Fruit Carving 13
Chapter 2: Fruit and Vegetable Carving Today 14
    Fruit Carving 14
    Vegetable Carving 15
    Famous Food Carving Artists 16
    Carl Franklin Jones 16
    Valeriano Fatica 16
    Jimmy Zhang 16
Chapter 3: Thai and Japanese Food Carving 17
    Thai Fruit Carving 17
    Thaeng Yuak 18
    Japanese Fruit Carving 19
Chapter 4: Essential Fruit & Vegetable Carving Tools 21
Chapter 5: The Best Vegetables & Fruits for Carving 25
    Tips in Choosing Fruits and Vegetables for Carving 27
    Preparing Vegetables and Fruits before Carving 29
    Storing Fruits and Vegetables after Carving

....30
Chapter 6: Step-by-step Guide to Fruit & Vegetable Carving 31
    How to Learn Fruit and Vegetable Carving 31
    Where to Find Fruit Carving Tutorials 33
    Step-by-step Simple Fruit Carving Instructions..34
        How to Make Carrot Flowers 34
        Shaping a Cucumber Leaf 35
        How to Carve a Watermelon into a Heart Basket 37
        Turning a Radish into a Flower 38
        Carving a Melon Bowl 39
        Carving a Pumpkin 43
        Making an Apple Swan......................... 46
        How to Make Strawberry Flowers 50
    Presenting Food Carvings............................ 54
Conclusion..55

Copyright

Copyright 2017 by Francine Agile All rights reserved.

This document is geared towards providing exact and reliable information in regards to the topic and issue covered. The publication is sold with the idea that the publisher is not required to render accounting, officially permitted, or otherwise, qualified services. If advice is necessary, legal or professional, a practiced individual in the profession should be ordered.

- From a Declaration of Principles which was accepted and approved equally by a Committee of the American Bar Association and a Committee of Publishers and Associations.

In no way is it legal to reproduce, duplicate, or transmit any part of this document in either electronic means or in printed format. Recording of this publication is strictly prohibited and any storage of this document is not allowed unless with written permission from the publisher. All rights reserved.

The information provided herein is stated to be truthful and consistent, in that any liability, in terms of inattention or otherwise, by any usage or abuse of any policies, processes, or directions contained within is the solitary and utter responsibility of the recipient reader. Under no circumstances will any legal responsibility or blame be held against the publisher for any reparation, damages, or monetary loss due to the information herein, either directly or indirectly.

Respective authors own all copyrights not held by the publisher.

The information herein is offered for informational purposes solely, and is universal as so. The presentation of the information is without contract or any type of guarantee assurance.

The trademarks that are used are without any consent, and the publication of the trademark is without permission or backing by the trademark owner. All trademarks and brands within this book are for clarifying purposes only and are the owned by the owners themselves, not affiliated with this document.

Introduction

Thank you for downloading this book!

This book is entitled, " Food Carving: Your Definitive Guide to Decorative Fruit and Vegetable Carving for All Occasions!

This book will give an in-depth discussion about the early beginnings and modern applications of food carving. It will provide information about the history of food carving and its origins from various countries.

This book will also give some useful tips on how to choose and prepare fruits and vegetables for carving. It will also teach you how to properly store fruit and vegetable carvings. It will also provide you with step-by-step instructions on how to make different kinds of fruit or vegetable carvings.

Keep on reading to learn more about food carving!

Chapter 1: The History of Food Carving

Carving was already popular even in the earlier times. Even prehistoric men carved images on surfaces, such as clay, stone, wood, soil, bark, bones, meat, leaves, fruits, dough, vegetable and even human flesh. It was a form of communication before it became an art. And one of the best ways of showcasing the skill of carving is through food carving.

Food carving is one of the many kinds of art forms. It is also one type of culinary skill. Many food products, such as dough, block of ice, rice, bread, fish, vegetable skin, fruit peel, leaves, and ribs can be used for food carving.

Though any fruit can be used for carving, some fruits and vegetables are more suitable for carving.

Soggy, soft and perishable fruits and vegetables are not recommended for food carving. The most suitable fruits or vegetables are watermelons, pumpkins, cantaloupes and apples.

There is a wide range of possibilities when it comes to food carving. The only problem with this fancy art is that food products can easily spoil and are delicate to handle. It is also difficult to preserve the artwork and make it last longer.

Fruit and Vegetable Carving

Fruit and vegetable carving is an art and skill on its own. One must be skillful and artistic enough to create such wonderful masterpieces from fruits and vegetables.

In carving vegetables and fruits, you need to use accuracy, skill and strategy in making a work of art. Unlike other materials, such as wood, bone and stone, mistakes made food carvings can never be reshaped or extremely difficult to alter.

In food carving, which is a very delicate version of wood carving, special tools are needed to achieve realistic and intricate designs. Some of the most commonly used tools in food carving are: melon baller, peel zester, paring knife, and "U" and "V" form cutters.

Ice Carving

Ice carvings are normally made during cold or winter season. It is one of the highlights in most winter events. The cold weather is most suitable in keeping the piece of ice carving in its perfect shape. Just like vegetable and fruit carving, ice carving requires skill, precision and specialized tools.

Tools for ice carving can range from chainsaws, ice chisels, and carving machines.

Rhythm and speed is needed to prevent the ice carving's natural melting process. The carver's ideas and execution must get along really well in order to create the desired design before the ice melts.

Tibetan Food Carving

Food carving is a part of religious and traditional Tibetan art, Torma. Butter sculptures are made during special occasions, such as Tibetan New Year. Yak butter and dye are used in creating butter sculptures. One of the largest food carving creation was made out of frozen butter.

History of Vegetable Carving

Vegetable carving has been practiced in several countries across Asia for a long time.

This is why the origin of vegetable carving remains unclear. Some people believe that it originated in China during the Tang (618-906 AD) and Song (960-1279 AD) dynasty. Others believe that it started in Thailand and Japan.

Japanese Vegetable Carving

Mukimono is an art that involves fruit and vegetable carving. It has been practiced in Japan for many years and is considered as the root of food carving.

Mukimono originated from the ancient times, when food was served in rough clay plates lined with a leaf. Creative chefs eventually discovered that the folding and cutting of the leaf will result into a more appetizing food presentation.

Mukimono finally became popular during the Edo period (16th century). Artistic food presentations were made by street food sellers. Eventually, the practice has become a part of professional chef's training in Japan.

Thai Vegetable Carving

Some people believe that vegetable carving originated in Thailand. It started in the 14th century during Loi Krathong festival. The festival showcases rafts that are decorated with flowers and banana leaves.

Nang Noppamart, one of King Phra Ruang's servants, made bird-shaped and flower-shaped vegetable carvings to decorate a raft for the festival. King Phra Ruang was very pleased by the creation that he decreed that every woman should learn the art of carving.

It was in 1808 when King Rama II showed his love for vegetable carving through poetry. However, the interest for vegetable carving waned over time. To revive this dying art, vegetable carving was taught in primary and secondary schools in Thailand.

Chinese Fruit Carving

There are also some accounts that the first fruit carvings were made in China during Tang dynasty (618-906 AD). Chinese fruit carvings commonly showcase animal forms and mythical creatures. They usually used fruit carvings for traditional rites and cultural ceremonies. They also used fruit carvings to impress guests during home visits and special occasions.

Fruit carvings were also used in China to tell stories and folklore. Watermelon is the most commonly used fruit in Chinese fruit carving. They scrape out the insides of the watermelon and create carvings on the outer part of the skin. It is also used as a bowl for flowers or fruits.

European Fruit Carving

Fruit carving was first featured in Europe on 1621. It was included in Matthias Giegher's work entitled "Il Trinciante" or The Carver. It depicted citrus fruits carved into shells, animals and abstract figures. It has become more popular in the 1980s when fruit carving books were already published.

Moreover, bread and pudding carvings with the use of molds were first seen in Babylon and Roman Britain.

Chapter 2: Fruit and Vegetable Carving Today

Fruit Carving

Today, fruit carving is becoming popular in art and culinary field. There are many professional fruit carvers around the world. There are also chefs who practice fruit carving to enhance their culinary practices.

Professional fruit carvers who have mastered many advanced carving techniques are paid well by caterers, restaurants, resorts and hotels. They provide beautiful centerpieces for large events like weddings and parties. They also make fruit carvings as garnishing to enhance food presentation and make it look more appealing to customers.

Vegetable Carving

Vegetable carving is popular in many Asian countries. It is commonly featured in cruises, restaurants, resorts and hotels. It has also become popular in other countries outside Asia during the mid-20th century. From then on, it has been well practiced and appreciated around the globe.

Vegetable carvings normally feature birds and flowers. However, many creative vegetable carvers have showcased other unique and intricate forms and figures in their masterpieces. The end result of vegetable carving may depend on the technique and creativity of the carver. Some artists can make simple but elegant vegetable carvings. Others can make intricate and detailed vegetable art. It is usually used as garnishing but it can also be used to make bouquets and table centerpieces.

Famous Food Carving Artists

There are a lot of restaurant chefs and professional food carvers in the world who have great fruit and vegetable carving skills. They use different skills and techniques in food carving. Some of them are already holding seminars and classes in food carving. The following are some popular food carvers in the world:

Carl Franklin Jones
He is an expert in fruit carving. He is a business man and artist based in the United States. One of his famous works was the fruit carving that he created for the wedding of Ivanka Trump. He also has a catering business in Tennessee. He is now traveling the world to hold programs and teach aspiring fruit carvers, chefs and artists.

Valeriano Fatica
He is an Italian fruit carver who became popular for his Youtube videos. His videos featured his art works, and was viewed by a lot of people around the world. He can carve a large-scale masterpiece that includes many different fruits.

Jimmy Zhang
He is a popular fruit carver from China. He has received several culinary awards. His skills has also been recognized by many newspapers around the world.

Chapter 3: Thai and Japanese Food Carving

Thai Fruit Carving

Thai fruit carving is an art that requires discipline, precision, neatness, ability and meditation. It has been a well-respected art in Thailand. It has been used to ornament table spreads of the Thai royal family. Women in the Thai royal palace were taught how to carve vegetables and fruits. It is also a traditional custom that is done during Songkran.

According to a legend, during Sukhothai era, a servant girl wants to create the most beautiful lantern. So she placed many flowers into her lantern. Then she carved fruits into swan and bird, and put them on top of the flowers.

Some skilled Thai carvers use only one knife in fruit carving. However, many kinds of tools can be used in making beautiful carvings. Some of these are: plane handle knife, round handle knife, crafting knife, scoop, peeler, molder, and scissors.

Thai fruit carvers use different kinds of fruits and vegetables in carving. They categorize it into thin and thick fruits.

The most common fruits that they use are: cucumber, carrot, radish, tomato, taro, chili, ginger, pumpkin, leek, lemon, lettuce, onion, beetroot, cabbage, papaya, apple, pineapple, guava, watermelon, cantaloupe, mango, yam, sapodilla, rose apple, dragon fruit and monkey apple.

Thaeng Yuak

Thaeng yuak is the Thai art of carving banana stalk. "Tang" means stab or carve, and "yuak" means banana stalk. Thaeng yuak is practiced during funerals, and religious and cultural ceremonies. There only a few Thaeng yuak artists.

Thaeng yuak is popular in Phetchaburi and Ayutthaya province in central Thailand. They usually use thaeng yuak to decorate funeral area and biers. It is a part of paying their respect to the dead. Remarkable personalities and well-known monks are offered with thaeng yuak made by skillful artists.

However, the popularity of this art is slowly decreasing because of foreign influences in Thai culture.

Japanese Fruit Carving

Mukimono is a popular art in Japan that involves creating decorative garnishing. The most common forms that are showcased in mukimono carvings are cranes, flowers, dragons and turtles. Vegetables, such as carrot, daikon and eggplant are also used to make twists, flowers and fan shapes. They are either served in small individual plates or as garnishing on meals.

Mukimono has helped in establishing Japan's national identity. Li Po, a Chinese poet, mentioned in his work that the Japanese won battles and received blessings from God through carving mythical shapes. Fruit carving became more popular during the Edo period (1603-1867).

Mukimono is inspired by the four seasons. Japanese artists believed that the harmony of flavors among the four seasons improve the overall taste of the cuisine, as well as its appearance.

The intricate design and skillful cutting of food brings delight to people who were served with mukimono. It also brings life and color to a table or banquet.

Mukimono makes the food more appealing and appetizing. Any kind of fruit or vegetable can be turned into a work of art by mukimono artists.

In earlier times, the Japanese use bare and unglazed bowls and plates in serving food. To make the food more appealing and impress the guests during festivities and special occasions, food servers place flowers, and fruit or vegetable carvings.

Japanese are skillful meat carvers. It was proven by their skills in making sushi and sashimi. Another proof is their creativity in arranging food on a plate or bento box. It is a fun and delightful way of serving food with the help of food carving.

Chapter 4: Essential Fruit & Vegetable Carving Tools

In order to make fruit and vegetable carvings, an artist must have the essential tools to create different artworks. The following tools are used in making food carvings:

Peel Zester

It is one of the helpful tools in fruit carving. It can make grooves and strips.

Paring knife

Paring knife is the most commonly used tool in fruit and vegetable carving. It is used in making different shapes. It is also called bird's beak knife. It has a sharp edge that bends inward. It is easily controlled by the hand.

'U' shaped garnishing tool

It is ideal for carving the internal part and removing outer skin of fruits. This can be used to create petals out of 'slitted' strawberry flesh.

Melon baller

It makes tiny round balls by scraping melon flesh.

"V" formed cutter

V cutter can be used to make apple swan. It can be used to make wings out of apple halves or slices.

Crinkle-Cut Blade

It is ideal for making wavy shapes. It is used for making wavy French fries.

Ceramic Knife

It is ideal for making very thin slices. It is non-reactive. It also stays razor sharp.

"V" Carving Knife

It is used for making V-shaped gouges.

Shape Cutters

It is smaller than cookie cutters. It can make different shapes.

Tourné Knife

It is quite smaller than paring knife. It can make delicate slices and cuts.

"U" Carving Knife

It is used for making U-shaped gouges.

Egg Cutter

It is used for slicing boiled eggs.

Scoopers

It has different sizes. It can be used for making holes and fruit balls.

Apple Corer/Curly Fry Maker

It is used to core and peel apples at the same time. It can also be used to make curly potato fries.

Wedger

It is used for making fruit and vegetable wedges.

Banana Slicer

It is used for making precise banana and fruit slices.

Vegetable Spaghetti Cutter

It is used to make curly strands and thin strands of vegetables, such as carrots and cucumbers. It is great for making nice salads and garnishing's.

Mandolin Slicer

It is very useful in any kitchen. It can be used for making paper thin slices of fruits, vegetables and meat. It can quickly make Julienne cut, wave, dice and cubes.

Food Carving Kit

As you can see from the above there are many different tools required for fruit & vegetable carving. If you are a beginner at this, I would recommend that you purchase an inexpensive kit with most of these tools from eBay already included. See image below.

Chapter 5: The Best Vegetables & Fruits for Carving

The necessary materials and tools must be prepared before carving a fruit. You have to make sure that all of the tools are within your reach before starting the process of carving.

There are two kinds of carving that can be practiced. The first one is "skin carving." It is the process of carving the skin of fruit or vegetable to reveal the inner part. It results into contrasting colors that emphasize the artistic design.

The second one is the "three-dimensional carving." It is the process of making a three-dimensional figure from the flesh of the fruit. The result will depend on the desire of the food carver. Flower pattern is the most common three-dimensional design. It is good outline the design before carving the whole fruit or vegetable.

Simple carving design may take a little time to finish. However, detailed and intricate design may need more time to accomplish.

When choosing vegetable and fruits for carving, opt for those that are fresh and have smooth skin. Do not choose overripe fruits and vegetables. These will be difficult to handle. It is also good to choose fruits and vegetables with bright colors. It will give better and more colorful finished product.

After buying fruits and vegetables, wash, dry and refrigerate it to keep it fresh.

Also make sure that the tools and knives are sharp before starting the process.

Take extra care when handling the fruits and vegetables.

Once the carving is done, wash the finished product with ice cold water. Cover it with cling wrap and store it in the fridge.

When stored well, this can keep for up to 4 to 7 days.

If you are displaying the carving in room temperature, you can spray ice cold water every now and then to keep it fresh.

If you are using vegetable (e.g. potato or apple) that changes its color once peeled, rinse it in cold water and vinegar/lemon juice solution.

Tips in Choosing Fruits and Vegetables for Carving

Radish - Choose medium-sized radish that is fresh, round and firm.

Onion/Shallot - Choose fresh and wrinkle-free onions of the same size. Small and medium-sized onion/shallots are more preferable for food carving.

Chinese Radish - Choose straight radish with clear skin. Opt for medium-sized radish because it is much easier to carve.

Carrots - Opt for medium to large carrots that is straight (not curved).

Tomato - Select fresh, wrinkle-free and uniform-sized tomatoes. Oblong-shaped plum tomatoes are firmer than round-shaped variety.

Cucumber - Green and straight cucumber is best for carving. When choosing small cucumber, opt for dark green skin. It has firmer flesh than light green cucumber.

Pumpkin - Choose pumpkin with rough skin. It should have firm flesh.

Spur Chili - Choose fresh spur chilies. It must have firm skin. Opt for small chilies for garnish and flowers. Opt for large chilies for large flowers.

Spring Shallot - Opt for green, fresh, thick and medium-sized shallots/leeks.

Taro - Opt for medium-sized taro.

Cabbage/Chinese Cabbage - Choose medium-sized, firm and heavy cabbage.

Lemon - Choose fresh lemon (not overripe).

Yam Bean - Do not choose large yam tubers because it has too much fiber and not ideal for carving.

Cantaloupe - Choose not fully ripe cantaloupe with firm and pale-yellow skin.

Green Mango - Choose fully mature green mango. Do not choose a mango with crisp flesh.

Watermelon - Choose watermelon that has firm skin and no bruises. The skin should be green and flesh should be red.

Papaya - Choose not fully mature papaya with firm skin and flesh.

Guava - Do not choose overripe guava. It should have no bruises.

Apple - Opt for fresh and shiny apple without bruises.

Pineapple - Opt for pineapple with large eyes and green leaves.

Sapodilla - Do not choose fully ripe sapodilla. The skin should be clear and even.

Rose apple - It should have clear and even skin.

Jujube - It should have no bruises and green skin. It should be straight.

Preparing Vegetables and Fruits before Carving

Soak tomatoes in water and lime juice solution to prevent oxidation.

Wash taro before peeling. It will release slime if washed after peeling, which can cause itching of your skin.

Soak onions and shallots in water before peeling and carving to avoid eye irritation.

Do not soak carrots in water before carving because water can make its flesh harder to carve.

Wash potatoes with water after peeling and after carving to prevent oxidation.

Wash beets with salt water to avoid change in color. Spray it with water from time to time to avoid blackening.

Soak apple in water and lime juice solution before peeling to avoid oxidation.

Wash cantaloupe before peeling. Once peeled, do not rinse because it will decrease its taste and speed up spoilage.

Storing Fruits and Vegetables after Carving

Do not put carved vegetables and fruits in water because it will spoil and ruin its color.

Spraying ice cold water can help keep fruit and vegetable carving firm.

Separate carved fruits according to type to avoid spoilage.

Quickly dip pumpkin in water after carving.

Store fruit and vegetable carving in separate containers and keep in the fridge.

If there is no refrigerator, wrap it in a thin damp cloth to avoid drying and wilting.

Chapter 6: Step-by-step Guide to Fruit & Vegetable Carving

How to Learn Fruit and Vegetable Carving

Attending a carving class is the most common means to learn fruit and vegetable carving. There are many Asian restaurants, culinary schools and chefs that conduct fruit and vegetable carving classes. It helps to find classes near your area from the internet. You can also look for online carving classes. It sends video tutorials for a minimal cost.

Buy the necessary carving tools. You need to buy vegetable peeler, paring knife, u-shaped knife, melon baller, v-shaped knife and others. These tools can make different kinds of patterns and cuts.

Carving tool sets are available online and at cooking supply stores. Having a knife sharpener will keep your knives sharp, and you can always make accurate carvings.

It is good to practice as often as you can. You can start by peeling fruits and vegetables, such as yams, apples, and cucumbers. Then, you can practice with your paring knife. Lastly, master how to use the v-shaped knives.

Paring knives can make straight and curved cuts. V-shaped knife can make clean and thin grooves. It can either make straight or curved lines.

Practice extra caution when handling knives. Carve away from your hand and fingers. Always sharpen your knives to avoid accident when it gets stuck on fruit and vegetable flesh.

Buying protective wood carving gloves can also help. It can protect your hand from getting cut by sharp knives.

Wash the knife handles when cutting slimy or juicy fruits and vegetables. This will prevent the knives from sliding from your hand.

Where to Find Fruit Carving Tutorials

If you want formal education, enroll in a culinary class that includes fruit and vegetable carving.

If you do not have enough money, there are online classes about fruit and vegetable carving. You can either enroll in an online class or watch free videos on YouTube.

If you watch enough videos, perhaps one day you will be this good:

Step-by-step Simple Fruit Carving Instructions

How to Make Carrot Flowers

Carrot flowers can be added to salads, drinks and stir-fry dishes. You only need knife, zester, peeler and cookie cutter to make some.

1. Peel and cut into thick slices.
2. Cut a few lengthwise wedges along the sides of each slice.
3. Cut the carrot pieces into thinner slices or coins.
4. You can also punch a hole in the center of each flower.
5. You will now have small carrot flowers.

Shaping a Cucumber Leaf

1. Prepare your carving tools. Get your carving knife, cutting board and cucumber.
2. The size of leaves depends on the size of cucumber.
3. Slice the cucumber into a wedge.
4. Slice the round end of the cucumber.
5. Cut the cucumber lengthwise diagonally.
6. Remove the seeds and excess flesh of cucumber.
7. Cut the wedge into a teardrop shape.
8. Place the cucumber on the cutting board.
9. Shape the end into a rounded point.
10. Carve a line in the center of the cucumber leaf. It will be the center vein.
11. Remove the green part and reveal the white inner part of the cucumber.
12. Carve lines along the sides of the center vein to make it look more like a leaf.

How to Make Watermelon Roses

1. Wash the watermelon.
2. Cut it into half. The halves must be equal in size.
3. Start working on one of the watermelon halves and set aside the other half.
4. Make a 1" thick slice by cutting it vertically.
5. Cut it into 4 equal pieces (just like a pizza).
6. Cut a square out of one piece (flesh only).
7. Make a letter "C" from this piece.
8. Make around 3 "C"s
9. Make 2 letter "V"s.
10. Then, make one "O."
11. You can now assemble it to make a rose shape.
12. Get the green part and carve a leaf shape.
13. Arrange the leaves and roses on a plate.

How to Carve a Watermelon into a Heart Basket

1. Choose a medium-sized watermelon.
2. Slice a small part at the bottom of the watermelon to make it more stable.
3. Make an outline (heart pattern) on the watermelon skin using a marker or pencil.
4. Cut the water melon into half.
5. Leave a thick part of the skin to use as a handle for the basket.
6. Decorate the edges of the remaining half while avoiding the handle.
7. Carefully remove the inner part/flesh of the watermelon and set aside.
8. Cut out small hearts from the removed skin and attach onto the basket with toothpicks.

Turning a Radish into a Flower

1. Prepare the materials and tools, such as radish, carving knife, v-shaped carving knife, and cutting board. Choose a medium radish with smooth skin. Its roots should be white and the tops should be green.
2. Remove the leaves from radish using carving knife. Keep the stalk because it can be used as a handle.
3. Start making the petals. Use the V shaped knife to carve the skin of radish to make pointed cuts. This can make triangular-shaped leaves on the flesh.
4. Carve one centimeter into the flesh to let the petals open.
5. Soak it in ice cold water for about an hour. This will let the petals open up naturally.

Carving a Melon Bowl

1. First, choose a melon with hard and firm skin. It should have no bruising.
2. Cut a small portion from the bottom of the melon. This will make it more stable for carving.
3. Use a bronze or stainless stell knife to prevent discoloration.
4. Make a pattern on the melon. Use a marker or pencil to make the pattern. You can draw swan head and wings. You may also use a stencil to make the pattern.
5. Though melon is not usually used for carving, you can adapt pumpkin and watermelon carving tutorials in carving melon.
6. Carve along the pattern on the melon. Insert the knife and follow the markings to create the design.
7. Sharp knives are easier to glide along the rind and flesh of melon. You can also cut little by little.
8. Once you have cut through the pattern, you may remove the excess rind.
9. Cut the top part of the melon to make an opening.
10. Remove the flesh from the insides of the melon. You can use a melon baller to remove the flesh of melon. You can remove the entire flesh or keep a thin layer.

11. Fill the bowl with fruit salad. You can also use it to hold trifles, small snacks and other food
12. You can drain the liquid from the salad before serving by making holes at the bottom of melon bowl

13. You can line the inside of the melon bowl with parchment paper if the bottom is too thin to hold the contents.
14. You can also turn the removed top of melon into a lid.

Carving a Cucumber Flower

1. Slice a section of cucumber.
2. Cut a large cucumber into three or a small cucumber into two.
3. The size is not important, but the piece you need to carve should include a close and open end.
4. Do not throw away other portions because you may need to repeat the process to do it perfectly.
5. Cut strips onto the skin just before the flesh.
6. Use a paring knife and put it on the edge of open end.
7. Slice it down about 1/8" deep from the skin.
8. Cut until 1/2" away from the close end.
9. Leave the strip of skin attached to the end.
10. Make strips around the cucumber.
11. If you fail, try it again on the other remaining portions.
12. Do this process on the flesh of the cucumber to make white inner petals.
13. Make the strips thick enough not to break and thin enough to bend.
14. Scrape the pulp and seeds carefully using a knife.
15. Remove remaining flesh that are not strips.

16. Trim the green part to make it pointed. Make the cut triangular and symmetrical.
17. Place a colorful accent at the center. You can use a carrot disc, tomato peel, or small berry. You can also add edible flowers, such as clover, dandelion buds or English daisy.

Carving a Pumpkin

1. Get pumpkin from pumpkin patch, supermarket or farmer's market.

2. Choose a pumpkin that has no cuts, nicks and bruises. Make sure that it has a sturdy stem. Make sure that it has an even color. You van thump or knock on the skin. A hollow sound means that the pumpkin is ripe.
3. Wash the pumpkin with a cloth once you get home. Keep it in a bucket of water to keep its moisture.
4. Pick your desired size. A larger pumpkin may need more work. If you are going to make an elaborate carving, choose a medium to large size. Small pumpkins are good for kids.
5. Pumpkin will rot after 7 to 14 days after picking so make sure that you buy a pumpkin about a week or less before the occasion.
6. Decide on the method that you will be using.
7. Some people carve the usual jack-o-lantern that has eyes, nose and mouth. It is advisable for beginners.
8. Some people make a silhouette and then eyes and mouth, where the light will pass through.

9. Some people carve just through the pulp. This works for pumpkins that don't intend to be lighted.
10. Advanced carvers use bas relief method. It includes carving through the skin, through the gourd and includes more difficult pattern. Posterized image can make the pattern easier to copy by the carver.
11. Use a permanent marker to draw the pattern on the pumpkin. Advanced carvers even use a projector to place the outline onto the pumpkin.
12. Children can help with drawing of patterns but not in the carving process,
13. A jab saw and serrated knife is appropriate for pumpkin carving. Make a back and forth motion when caving the pumpkin. Do not use straight-edged knives. Those are difficult to use in carving pumpkins.
14. Work in a spacious area. Line the floor with brown sack or newspapers. This will protect the surface and cleaning up will be much easier.
15. Prepare your tools and a bowl for discarding pumpkin pulp and gourd.
16. Make a lid. Cut the top portion of the pumpkin at around 2" from the stem.

Cut it in a way that it will stay in place or rest into the center of the pumpkin.

17. Remove the lid and clean the inner part by scraping the gourd and flattening its bottom.
18. You can also make a lid with a star or square shape.
19. Scrape the inner parts of the pumpkin. You can use your hands or a spoon to scrape it. Clean the insides as you can to let more light shine through the carved pattern.
20. This should only be done if you are going to light the pumpkin.
21. You can cut the bottom of the pumpkin if it does not stand on its own.
22. As you carve the design, discard the cut out skin and flesh into the bowl.
23. You can use candle, tea lights or LED lights to light your pumpkin.

Making an Apple Swan

1. Buy a large apple.
2. Buy an apple that can stand up straight.
3. Any variety of apple will do but it is good to choose a large apple.
4. Cut the center of the apple in a slight angle.
5. Stand it upright and remove the core.
6. Remove the seeds of the apple and set it aside for later.
7. Put two butter knives on each side of the apple.
8. Lay the apple flat on the cutting board.
9. Put the two butter knives perpendicular at the base of the apple.
10. This will act as a stopper so that you will never cut through the entire apple.
11. Slice the right of the apple core vertically about 1/2" wide.
12. Make a wedge by slicing the apple horizontally.
13. Do the same at the other side of the apple.
14. Make wedges on both sides of the apple.
15. There should be a thin body at the center of the apple.
16. Place the two knives on both sides of the apple wedge.

17. Lay the apple wedge on its flat side between the two knives. The knives must be at the top and bottom of the apple wedge.
18. Cut a 1/4" of vertical cut through the apple wedge.
19. Slice a vertical cut 1/4" from the flat side of the wedge.
20. Keep making cuts until the knives stop you.
21. Flip the wedge over.
22. Make another vertical cut.
23. Flip the apple on the other flat side and make another vertical cut.
24. This will make another smaller wedge from the larger wedge of apple.
25. Repeat the method two times on the smaller wedges.
26. Place the smaller piece between the knives and make another wedge.
27. Repeat the method until you made three or more different sized apple wedges.
28. These will be the different layers of the swan's wings.
29. Arrange the pieces of apple to make wings on the body.
30. Push out the apple wedges so that they look like wings.
31. Each wedge must show a little part of wedge under it to appear like a wing.
32. Do the same process on the other apple wedge so that you have two wings.

33. Slice a 1/2" slot from the middle of the body.
34. Using a small knife, cut out 1/2" wide rectangle and 3/4" deep.
35. Slice the remaining side of the apple.
36. Place two knives adjacent to the other half of the apple.
37. Create a full horizontal slit through the bottom of your apple. This should make a thin slice of apple that can be used for the swan's head and should look like a heart.
38. Get the slice of apple and create two diagonal cuts to make a V.
39. Get the flat slice that you made and create two diagonal slits near the upper right of the slice. This will be the head.
40. Imagine what a swan's head is like.
41. You can use photos from the internet so that you can make a nice swan's head and neck.
42. Make a straight slit on the bottom for the base.
43. Finish the head by making a cut on one side of the apple slice, just below the V that you cut.
44. You can refine the appearance of the swan head by cutting it more.
45. You can smoothen rough angles using a small knife around the neck and head to make it more realistic.
46. Place the apple seeds to make the eyes.

47. Using a butter knife, press the seeds into the apple.
48. Fit the neck into the slot that you made.
49. Place the swan head into the rectangular slot.

How to Make Strawberry Flowers

Strawberries can be carved into flowers and arranged into beautiful and delicious bouquets. Choose large strawberries with a bright red color. Make sure that the strawberries are firm. Uniform size strawberries look better.

1. Rinse and dry the strawberries before making the flowers.
2. You will need one skewer to handle the strawberry while cutting the petals into it.
3. Use a small paring knife for cutting. Sharpen the paring knife before carving the strawberry.
4. Push the strawberry's base into the skewer.

5. It is the end of strawberry with leaves.
6. This can keep the strawberry in place while creating the flower.
7. Make the outer petals.
8. Use a paring knife to cut a small section of the strawberry downwards going to the stem about 1/4 inch deep.
9. You will be able to make four to six petals around the bottom of the strawberry depending on its size.
10. After you making the cuts, use the flat side of the paring knife to bend the petals outwards, so it should curls like a flower.
11. Make more layers of flower petals to the strawberry.
12. You must be able to make about three to four sets of petals on the strawberry.
13. Continue creating slight cuts around the strawberry.
14. Each row should have fewer petals as you continue upwards.
15. As you cut towards the top, make the cuts as thin and as close to the skin of strawberry as possible.
16. It will let the petals curl outwards and appear more realistic.
17. You can also add chocolate.

18. You can make the strawberry flowers into a treat or special gift by adding a sweet drizzle of melted dark, white or milk chocolate.
19. For a more decadent and solid look, you can dip the strawberry flowers completely in melted chocolate.
20. To make an even chocolate drizzle, transfer your melted chocolate into a small plastic bag.
21. Cut off one corner of the bag slightly to make a small hole.
22. Squeeze the bag and drip the chocolate onto your strawberry flower as if you are piping icing.
23. Spread out your strawberries on parchment or wax paper to let the chocolate set and avoid smudging and mess. so that it doesn't become messy or smudged.
24. You can also make it look classy by adding edible pearls in the petals. This can add a touch of color and sparkle. Sugar pearls are available in baking supplies.
25. You can use melted chocolate as a glue for the sugar pearls. Let the chocolate dry completely before moving the strawberry flowers.

26. You can also add colorful sprinkles into the strawberries. Kids really like sprinkles especially when it comes with chocolate.
27. Dip the strawberry on melted chocolate before adding sprinkles.
28. You can also drizzle it with melted chocolate before adding the sprinkles.
29. Let it dry on parchment or wax paper.
30. You can also use flower stems to skewer the strawberry flowers to make it into a realistic bouquet.
31. You can also dye the skewers using green food color and let it dry before using.
32. Put the strawberry flowers in a flower vase to make a delectable fruit carving.

Presenting Food Carvings

A fruit bowl made from melon or watermelon is a popular way of presenting carved fruits. Fill it with fruit balls and cut ups to showcase a colorful fruit salad.

Strawberries, blueberries, cantaloupes and watermelon look good together.

Avoid raspberries because these can easily bruise.

Serving fruit carving in a platter made of glass, ceramic or wood is also recommended. The large carvings should be at the center. The small fruits should be around the edges of the platter.

Fruit carvings can also be presented in a bouquet, secure the bottom of the vase by putting floral foam. Skewer the vegetables and fruits using bamboo sticks. Put the sticks of fruits and vegetables into the vase.

Cherry tomatoes, grapes and cut up fruits are nice to include in a fruit bouquet. You can also put some lettuce to add some contrast.

Conclusion

There you have it!

I hope that you enjoyed reading this book. By now, I am sure that you are already equipped with useful knowledge about fruit and vegetable carving.

I encourage you to try fruit and vegetable carving as a new hobby and skill. With all of the things you have learned from this book, I am sure that your table centerpieces and food presentations will always be more exciting and impressive!

www.ingramcontent.com/pod-product-compliance
Lightning Source LLC
LaVergne TN
LVHW021014120125
801057LV00009B/849